Having worked for many years in both conventional and alternative education, Lindsay Clarke is a freelance writer living in Somerset, whose work has been widely translated. His novel *The Chymical Wedding* won the Whitbread Fiction Award in 1989 and more recently *The Water Theatre* was long-listed for the IMPAC Dublin International Literary Award. He is an Associate of the MA Creative Writing Programme at Cardiff University and Creative Consultant to the educational work of the Pushkin Trust in Northern Ireland.

for Crysse
with love
and all good wishes

Lindsay

Also by Lindsay Clarke:

Sunday Whiteman
The Chymical Wedding
Alice's Masque
Essential Celtic Mythology
Parzival and the Stone from Heaven
The War at Troy
The Return from Troy
The Water Theatre
Stoker
Imagining Otherwise
The Gist: A Celebration of the Imagination

A Dance with Hermes

LINDSAY CLARKE

Lindsay Clarke

AWEN
Stroud

First published in 2016 by Awen Publications
12 Belle Vue Close, Stroud GL5 1ND, England
www.awenpublications.co.uk

Front cover image: Kylix, cup, Attic, Attica, Vulci
© The Trustees of the British Museum
Reproduced by permission of the British Museum

Extract from John Moat, *Anyway ...*, privately published
© Antoinette Moat
Reproduced by permission of Antoinette Moat

Cover design by Kirsty Hartsiotis

ISBN 978-1-906900-43-4

Remembering

John Moat

(1936–2014)

Tetelesmenoi Hermei

Anyway … there was a small round pond in the garden, crammed with water lilies, and not to be fallen into because of its uncharted stagnant depths. In the centre set on a stone was a two-foot statue of Mercury. So the point is he was there from the outset … and that his being there, set on the stone in the pond, signified (or rather signifies because such matters exist in the exclusive present) that I had been fingered by Mercurius. How can I be so sure? Because to those who have been so fingered, things happen. Things you wouldn't notice if you hadn't been fingered.

John Moat, Anyway…

I should imagine that the name *Hermes* has to do with speech, and signifies that he is the interpreter (*hermeneus*), or messenger, or thief, or liar, or bargainer: all that sort of thing has a great deal to do with language.

Plato, Cratylus *(trans. Benjamin Jowett)*

CONTENTS

FOREWORD

The ancient Egyptian priests devoted their lives to animating the statues of their gods: dressing them in fine robes, leaving food at their feet, painting precise portraits and, especially, telling their stories – what they said and did and why they were gods at all. This was a celebration in itself, but it may also have served to draw the gods out of the forms in which we haplessly imprison them, so their essential natures might become more distinct.

Lindsay Clarke's *A Dance with Hermes* steps effortlessly into that noble tradition, bringing the elusive Hermes brilliantly and vividly to life, dreaming the myth onwards in an entirely new and exciting way. The forty-nine poems, together with the introduction and the notes to individual poems at the end, offer a unique guide to Hermes' multiple guises and disguises and the playful irony of his underlying purposes. Clarke brings his considerable erudition and love of language to allow the intellectual and the poetic mind to come together, imagining where and how Hermes might be concealed in everyday life – the whisper in the inner ear, the sudden silence when 'the air hangs watchful', or 'the fitful flare that lights our way'.

So past and present become translucent to each other. Clarke follows Hermes from his escorting of Priam to Achilles' tent, through the dreams of any age, to alchemy; from hermeneutics to the internet; from Psychopomp to teenage hacker – wherever there is a messenger, a trickster, anything shape-shifting, double-dealing, 'playing hide and seek'.

Writing poems about the source of poetry makes it even more likely that the form will find the writer. As Clarke says: 'it presented itself in four quatrains held together by the regular use of half-rhymes … with occasional full rhymes echoing on his sudden presence'. He plays formidably with his rhymes throughout, in tones that are both teasing and serious, parodic, admiring, yet mocking and deeply respectful all at once – an achievement in the art of 'polymetis' (skilled in many things, many of them incompatible and some of them wise) worthy of the god himself.

In turn, we may ask: is Clarke challenging what he calls the god's 'essential ambiguity' by beguiling him into the formality of rhymes, half or full? Yet, by momentarily pinning him down, Clarke is surely provoking the god to reveal himself more particularly for our modern age – to show what William Blake calls 'the bounding line' – and keeping him there just long enough for us to catch a glimpse of him before – like a breeze in autumn, like a mist – he is gone.

Jules Cashford

A NOTE AT THE THRESHOLD

Like the idiosyncratic nature of the ancient deity it celebrates, this little book is something of an oddity. At first glance it might appear to be a collection of poems or, possibly, a single long poem divided into individual bite-size sections. A closer reading may well lead some readers to question whether its contents are poetry at all, but rather, as its editor suggested, a narrative argument – sometimes co-medic, sometimes grave – conducted in verse, around a single enig-matic theme. Perhaps it is all of these things, or none of them, or both at the same time – which is to say that it's a betwixt-and-between, threshold sort of creature, mischievous, equivocal and nonchalant about boundaries and definitions. Which is perhaps also to say that, in that respect, it resembles the liminal nature of its tute-lary spirit, Hermes himself.

Whatever else it may be, as far as its author is concerned this book started life as a 'hermaion', which is the name, derived from that of Hermes, that the Greeks gave to what we call a 'windfall' or, more aptly, a 'godsend'. It happened this way.

In the closing months of a terminal illness my friend, the poet and novelist John Moat, completed an extraordinary memoir titled *Anyway ...*, which I was privileged to read. It's a moving, insightful, often funny, beautifully worded account of a life lived in service of the Imagination, which John equated with the activity of the wing-heeled god because he understood it as a power much larger than our human share in it. In one form or another, Hermes seems to have presided over much of his life from the childhood moment when he first encountered the small statue of Mercury in his parents' garden, and on through significant coincidence after coincidence, journey after journey, and chance meeting after meeting, throughout his 78 years – including the charmed set of circumstances which led to the foundation and growth of the magnificently successful Arvon writing courses.

So engagingly is the figure of Hermes conjured in John's memoir that it left me feeling impelled to try to write a poem about the god. I included it with the letter I wrote to him and John rang me shortly afterwards saying, 'Hmm, that looks like the start of something new!' What he had read was 'Koinos Hermes', the first of the following procession of poems, verses, squibs – call them what you like – and to my astonishment it turned out that he was right.

That poem conflates attributes of the Greek Hermes with those of Mercurius Duplex, the agent of transformation in alchemy, while at the same time making use of anachronistic contemporary references and colloquialisms. It presented itself in four quatrains held together by the regular use of half-rhymes to suggest the elusive nature of the god – something almost grasped but not quite – with occasional full rhymes echoing on his sudden presence. Though I didn't know it at the time, it had provided a format that became more or less standard for the sequence of verses which followed hot on its winged heels almost by dictation.

One by one the verses accumulated, rather like the stones placed by the ancient Greeks on the cairns (which they called 'hermae') at crossroads or to indicate where the next water source could be found. Unexpected, unplanned, but certainly welcome, Hermes had entered the house, proceeded to blow breezily about the place and left in his wake this hermaion which you are holding in your hands.

The experience of being the vehicle for its delivery left me convinced that, for all our attempts to understand the process of creativity, it remains mysterious. Thinking about it, I sometimes visualise the cranium as a kind of crystal ball inside which a whole galaxy of neurons ceaselessly flash and sparkle as they transmit messages across the synapses at quantum speed, constantly trading images, energy and information between the outer world and the inner world and over the porous boundary between the conscious and unconscious minds. That image reminds me of Hermes, the messenger god of thresholds and trade, travelling invisibly about his business of negotiation and exchange between our human world and the world of the gods. He is a deity with so many attributes and functions that he seems to resume in his own shape-shifting character the subtle polytheistic nature of the whole archetypal pantheon of gods which the Greeks placed on Mount Olympus, but whom we have come to understand as potential energies that, in the words of William Blake, 'reside in the human breast'.

Those gods are immortal because they remain active in every generation, presiding over the impersonal forces – love, sex, power and death among them – which James Joyce regarded as the 'grave and constant' themes of human life; though it might be truer to say that they remain active in every generation because they are immortal. And it follows that if they are constant and immortal then they don't change over time. But what does, can and must change is the nature of the way we perceive them; and that will alter our relations with them.

Such changes of perspective seem to reflect evolutionary shifts in the inflections of our consciousness, which do not, I think, imply *progress* in the Victorian understanding of that word, any more than that sort of progress is evident in the arts, where such shifts of perspective are perhaps most readily visible. But I think we can also see them at work in the way the ancient Greeks' perceptions of the god Hermes evolved over the course of hundreds of years.

The story of his debut among the Olympians is beautifully told in the Homeric Hymn to Hermes, which was composed not by Homer but by the Boeotian school of peasant poets around the seventh century BC. The *Iliad* and the *Odyssey*, both featuring the presence of Hermes, were composed around a hundred years before that, and the first surviving mention of him can be traced back much further to the Cretan Linear B tablets scribed about 1000 BC. Yet Hermes appears in the Hymn to his name not as a wise old man of great age, but as a newborn babe, a love child sired by Sky-Father Zeus on the shy nymph Maia where she lived in seclusion from the world in a cave on Mount Kyllene in Arcadia. He is presented therefore as a relative latecomer among the Olympians, and it's that peculiar fact which, along with other elusive aspects of his nature, makes him an oddity. For Hermes arrives at this very late stage of his history as something new – a baby, yes, but a baby who lay in his mother's womb for ten months and emerged from it endowed with extraordinary powers.

The many praise names by which Hermes was known to the Greeks are an index of those powers. Among a thesaurus of other titles, he was known to the ancient Greeks as Angelos Athanaton, messenger of the deathless gods; as Diaktoros, a guide, watching over travel; as Agathopoios, he who makes good, meaning 'procreative' or 'fertile'; and as Agoraios he was supervisor of the marketplace. The name Khrysorrhapis – he of the golden wand – points to his staff, the Kerykeion or Caduceus, which brings about magical transformations and is therefore an emblem of the imagination. He was called Psithyristis, the whisperer, referring to the inwardly mentoring voice of the daimon. He was also Eriounes, the bringer of luck; and as Psychopompos, guide of souls, he was present at every death to lead each shade across the asphodel fields into the underworld kingdom of Hades.

These and more are significant attributes of the Hermes who was counted among all the gods as the friendliest to men. But the Greeks were also well aware of his untrustworthy shadow side. To address him as Mekhaniotes, the contriver, was to praise his ingenuity, but it also carried a wary recognition of his cunning; so he was also known as Polytropos, meaning 'shifty', and as Pheletes, a thief, and Klepsiphron, a trickster and deceiver. Despite this disreputable behaviour, perhaps even because of it, he occupied a special place in the hearts of the Greeks, who also knew him affectionately as Koinos Hermes, the ordinary or commonplace god, the god who was to be found everywhere.

That they recognised so many impersonal powers at work through him suggests that the ancient Greeks well understood that the young Hermes who entered the Homeric world of the Olympian gods brought with him deep-rooted associations and attributes from a far earlier age. In any case, there is always an essential ambiguity in the nature of this god of the stone pile. He may be there as an invaluable guide across difficult terrain but he is not entirely to be trusted and may also choose to lead us astray. Hikers and climbers still add herm-stones to cairns, and Hermes still often faces us with choices at a crossroads; but as the image evolved in ancient times, instead of a rough stone pile, a monolith was erected in some terminal places, and a bearded head was carved on the standing stone, and out of its limbless pillar was thrust a vigorous penis. Here was Hermes as the god of fertility, drawing generative power up from the dark underworld – an ithyphallic alpha male, formidably guarding his herds beside the life-giving female presence of a spring.

In those places where a herma marked that liminal space which is a boundary between territories, people would have made a market for the exchange of goods, either using the silent trade or through interpreted languages. Boundaries, trade, sexual interaction, cheating, the complexities of language and the need for go-betweens – many aspects of the god, including (human nature being what it is) a talent for theft and swindling, must have manifested there. As the primitive images of him evolved, so too did human consciousness of him. By the time of his appearance in the Hymn to Hermes (of which Jules Cashford presents us with a graceful translation in the Penguin Classics) it's as if an urgently felt need for a new perspective on the god – a rebirth of his indispensable, subversive energy in subtler, more inflected form – had burst through into the Greek imagination and found exuberant expression.

Among the powers that the newborn god immediately assumes in the Hymn is that of imaginative invention. Thus, where others may have seen only a tortoise nibbling at the grass, Hermes sees the shape of a lyre, and the thought resonates in his mind as the possibility of music. It's a fine example of that 'double vision' – the simultaneous apprehension of literal fact and transformative insight – which Blake saw as the essence of imaginative energy. And having invented the lyre, Hermes immediately goes on to sing a song in praise of his father, his mother and his home. He does it, says the Hymn, in the same way that 'a quick thought darts through the heart of man'. We have already seen that this extraordinary, ordinary god was credited with inventing language; now we hear him singing the very first song, which means that in the same creative moment he invented poetry too.

The lyre and poetry are often associated with Phoebus Apollo, the god who was Hermes' elder brother, but we are assured by the Hymn that their origin does not lie with the Apollonian archetype. According to the vision – perhaps one should say the *re*-vision – from which the Hymn sprang, music and lyric poetry were both primary acts of the *Hermetic* imagination. Moreover, this is the first occasion on which Hermes uses his voice, so the myth also suggests that it is with Hermes that we will find the roots of language, not in prose but in poetry. One might go still further and say that this extraordinary, ordinary god is offering us a powerful archetypal image of the poetic basis of mind.

That phrase 'the poetic basis of mind' is, of course, in true Hermetic fashion, a theft. It's lifted from the Archetypal Psychologist James Hillman, whose wise post-Jungian imagination insisted on the primacy of images over concepts as a means of illuminating the operations of the soul, and on polytheistic mythology being both the rich source of such images and the primary guide to those operations. In that respect Hermes has figured timelessly throughout the course of European cultural history. Among Gnostic philosophers of the early Christian centuries he was honoured as Hermes Trismegistus, 'thrice-greatest', the originator of what was to develop into the Hermetic tradition of thought. He was familiar to Arabic scholars in that guise and proved vital to the revival of Neoplatonism by Marsilio Ficino and the Renaissance Academy of Florence. In the occult world of the alchemists he was revered as Mercurius Duplex, symbolising the elusive prime matter of their work and its final transmutation into the Philosophic Stone. More recently, through his profound study of densely imagistic alchemical texts which he had previously considered to be nonsensical, C. G. Jung was able to recognise and describe crucial aspects of the archetypal structure of the human psyche, thus further enlarging our awareness of the role of the unconscious in our lives.

It seems that Hermes reappears among us again and again, in slightly different but clearly related forms, and always to provoke imaginative thought while subtly refining our understanding of the complex, ambiguous creatures we deeply are.

So what about today? By harnessing the dizzying world of quantum physics through the astonishing technological achievements that generate, among other things, a proliferating exchange of emails, online international trade and banking, satellite navigation and the burgeoning influence of wide-reaching social media, the present age seems in many respects to be purpose-built for the unrestricted play of the Hermetic spirit. But the myths show us how shifty and unpredictable that spirit can be, and the wisdom of the ages asks what it will profit us if, in the process of gaining technocratic control of the world, we lose touch with our soul. My own suspicion is that, even as Hermes inspires the ingenious devices that evolve these days with algorithmic efficiency, he could prove sceptical of such technological literalisations of his essentially symbolic nature. After all, he is also Hermes Psychopompos, the guide of souls between this world and the next, a figure intermediate between life and death, who has a daimonic aspect that weighs our souls in the balance as the true determiner of our destinies.

Hermes is dancing about us everywhere these days, but largely unrecognised and perhaps, therefore, demanding a wider, more engaged imaginative response than he has so far been given. However, these threshold reflections have been conducted in conceptual prose, which always tends towards abstraction. The soul has a preference for images over concepts because its native tongue is poetry, which speaks from the heart to the heart through the senses and is the deep substrate of the mind from which our most deeply satisfying sense of meaning flows. So enough of this! Hermes is tapping his winged feet impatiently. It's time to join the dance.

Lindsay Clarke

Koinos Hermes

The work begins and ends with him: the sly
light-fingered god of crossways, transit,
emails and exchange, the wing-heeled, shifty,
wheeler-dealing go-between, who'll slip right

through your fingers if you try to pin
him down. For he is labile, street-wise
and trans-everything. He is the one
two-fold hermaphrodite who'll rise

up sprightly from the earth and turn to air,
and then descend into the underworld
to point his wand at philosophic gold.
You'll find him anywhere and nowhere,

ever the unexpected messenger, who sends
you glimpses of the wet fire and the lit dark
in the loded stone. With him the magic work,
of which one may not speak, begins and ends.

His Conception

Zeus Almighty, randy top Olympian
and father-of-it-all, is making secret love
to shy-eyed Maia in her mountain cave,
and thinking to himself he needs a son

to stir things up, a lad who has the nerve
to broker deals then take evasive action,
or to double-bluff, confusing fact and fiction
with a wily measure of inventive verve.

He thinks: *A world that's short on guile
and roguery lacks humour too. Let's have
a trickster then, who'll spin a line to save
divine appearances.* With such his will

(and goodwife Hera well deceived),
he thrusts … until a bright, illicit spark
of his imagination shoots into the fork
of Maia's loins, and Koinos Hermes is conceived.

His Birth

Then Zeus, of course, takes off. He's done his bit,
the seed is set, and who (apart from Hera) dare
berate his promiscuity. And Maia? Unaware
what trouble soon will batten on her teat,

she's lying peacefully asleep, and dreams
Sky-Father Zeus has filled her womb with love.
Zeus reckons what he's fathered is a knave,
a wag whose wits will improvise slick schemes

for trade-offs in diplomacy. The child
meanwhile is plotting out his destiny.
Impatient, sassy and precocious, he
is outward bound; his DNA is wild

and twisted like two snakes around a rod.
Ten months go by. Already itching for his wand
and wings, he leaps into the space beyond
his mother's womb … to find out he's a god.

First Steps

His mother sleeps, exhausted by the long night's work
of labouring a god into the world. Dawn breaks.
Laid snug inside a wicker basket, Hermes wakes
and stretches, yawns, then hears a morning lark.

At once he's restless. Eager and wide-eyed,
this babe won't miss a trick. He knows
a tasty world is waiting, so he puffs and grows
into a frisky boy who's up and off ... Outside,

he steps into the frosty mountain light
that glances off the snow, and what he sees
he likes. The thought of travelling agrees.
Wings flutter at his heels. He's out of sight.

Arcadia unfolds beneath him as he flies
from peak to peak. Alert, unboundaried,
he thinks, *That's it! – one day I'll be a guide
across a world where every map tells lies.*

Tortoise Song

But something's missing – music that will strum
the air and make a soundtrack for his flight.
No iPods yet, no Spotify – the world must wait
till he invents them, but the time has come

for entertainment of the ears. So what will pass?
He makes a banking turn down through the air,
glides back to land outside the cave, and there
he spots a tortoise nibbling at the grass.

A light-bulb moment this! He picks it up,
admires the polished pattern on its shell,
then scoops the creature out. This will
become his Stratocaster once he's cut

some strings and tuned them with a pick.
A bit more work. He plucks a note and likes
the sound. The tortoise sings. He strikes
a chord, sets generations dancing at the trick.

First Caper

That first day's dusk draws on. He's cruising high
above a mountain meadow where a herd
of long-horned cattle graze ... And there's no guard
in sight ... He thinks, *All property*

is theft: these might as well be mine,
and swoops to round them up, driving the whole
herd backwards to confuse the trail ...
For luck he sacrifices two fat kine,

then hides the rest, and heads for home.
But Maia, smelling cow-fat on his skin,
demands to know just what the boy has done.
(It's bound, she's sure, to damage her good name.)

He acts the innocent; then has the cheek to boast
he'll get away with it. She warns, 'Those cows,
were from Apollo's herd, and once he knows
who took them, boy, he'll have your tongue on toast!'

He Cuts a Deal

The lad's a larcenist. What's worse he blows
a fart right in Apollo's face. And no, the god
won't overlook this slight: he's after blood.
He'll teach this brat to rustle sacred cows.

But if the culprit is a god as well, what then?
He gets arraigned before the court of Zeus
where plaintiff and accused both plead their case.
Apollo feels quite confident he'll win

against this cocky boy, but then discovers that the judge
(his dad) is Hermes' father too, and may prefer
this newer son. The god of reason thinks it's clear
that right is on his side. He's not about to budge

no matter how persuasively the fibber talks …
But then he hears him strum his lyre. Enchanted
by that thrilling sound, he finds he's always wanted
such a thing. A deal is cut. And Hermes, smiling, walks.

He Considers Career Opportunities

A hotshot dealer on the trading floor?
He'd make a killing there, then break the bank.
Or he could ape it as a pop star for a prank
or rouse the rabble as a Red Top editor.

A life in crime could also see him thrive
as con-artist, or dip, or hacking phones,
and if as contract hit-man making bones
they sent him to the chair … well, he'd survive

as death's no problem. He could still return
at will to lead or lure, to hinder or abet.
One day he might upgrade the laggard internet
or play roulette with particles at CERN.

Right now he's temping for the Deity
as errand boy, ambassador and spy,
a trouble-shooting double, one who'll fly
on stand-by just to mystify the laity.

A PR Man Speaks Up

'If I may just put in a word ... I'm sure this client
welcomes such renewed attention to his fame,
but grows concerned that his good name's
at risk. I feel your verse is overly reliant

on bits of the Homeric Hymn – like some old file
that headlines all his juvenile delinquencies –
the cattle theft, the fart, the bare-faced lies.
But this god boasts much finer qualities than guile,

so shouldn't more respect be shown
for a divinity who's always tried
to serve the higher good that hides
behind misfortune? He is, of course, well known

both as a helpful friend and guide to men, as one
who leads them into sleep and brings
instructive dreams. And there's another thing ...'
But Hermes sighs, 'Oh do shut up! Sit down!'

An Alternative Version

An ancient lady, listening to a young bard
sing the Hymn to Hermes, raised her brows and smiled
to hear the tale of how Apollo's cattle herd
was deftly rustled by a newborn child.

'An entertaining story, yes,' she said, 'but just
a bit far-fetched! What babe has strength enough
for such a feat? This is new-fangled stuff!
I have an older tale to tell, one you can trust

because they told it in Mycenae and in Crete
a thousand years ago. Their Hermes was a god
of flocks, of wanderers and sex, who *made things good*
with his strong magic ... Look in any street,

you'll see some age-old image of him standing there
in silence boasting what he's truly famous for:
bearded, four-square, proud and perpendicular,
he is the stone with an erection at your door.'

His Better Nature

Unscrupulous? Disreputable? Yes ...
but never only that. He is the friendly angel
looking after crowd-lost kids, the stranger
who points out the way or helps you sort a mess

then vanishes. He's famous for evasiveness,
which has its charm. His wit is smart, ironical,
and sexy too. Just ask the nymphs: they'll tell
you how he'll smile a come-on, then confess

he has to keep another date; and yet his less
still somehow feels like more. And should he pull
a fast one on you, he's a grifter you'll recall
with half a smile at his glib wiliness.

He's handy too at setting up coincidence –
that timely contact met, the tip you overheard,
the winning ticket found when times were hard ...
This god's the choreographer of circumstance.

His Darker Side

But look, not even deathless gods can be complete
without a shadow in the soul, and Hermes gives
himself free rein round questions of morality.

Ever an opportunist, should he chance to meet
a lovely nymph ... well, she's fair game, and he believes
Chione is quite wrong to value her virginity

above all else. But she resists. It drives him wild.
He won't use force, of course. He'd rather wave
his magic wand and send her peacefully to sleep

to ease the rape. He gets the nymph with child
and, once awake, the wretched mother can't believe
how her unwanted son behaves. It makes her weep

to watch him trick and thieve. And yet Autolycus can grin
at all the upsets he creates – his dad will always keep
him safe from punishment. In fact, he's rather proud of him.

Dancing with Hermes

Is it just the winged buskins, or his thighs'
lithe muscularity, or his kinetic stance
that makes his godly body seem to dance
where others merely walk? Hermes defies

the laws of gravity and time and space,
and in the single batting of an eye
he'll wink and stamp his heels and fly
into a pirouette that startles with its grace.

And then he's gone, across wide land or sea
at Zeus's bidding or an impulse of his own.
Like a flash in darkness or the shine in rain,
swifter than quantum light-shifts, he

can leave you standing in an awestruck trance …
And yet imagination travels quite
as fast, so why not free it to take flight
and rise to follow Hermes in the dance?

He Knows What He Needs

He's not a singleton. Always there are
other divinities at hand, keeping
a watchful eye, or caught out unaware.
No god is left alone to do his thing

without some timely goddess chiming in
to complicate the game. She'll keep
his errant soul from falling fast asleep
because she's certain that its lamp will dim

if once it gets benighted by the mighty
algorithms of his intellect. He needs
that quickened sense of mystery which breeds
the healthy pedigree he shares with Aphrodite …

So when he starts to shake his golden wand
to activate some needful change in things,
he'll do so with the grace a naiad brings
to shape the flow of water with her hand.

He Cocks a Snook at Nietzsche
(and Philip Larkin)

Not those shiny minds that serve only Apollo,
nor passion addicts groggy from the vine
of Dionysos – neither of those types will swallow
Hermes' lines or let him subtly undermine
the rites and precepts of the gods they follow.

But being versatile, and keeping sharp his wits, he
sidles through the vacant slot between
their gods, then leaves them sitting pretty
while he cuts capers in that space, unseen,
and plunders and refines their rich myth-kitty.

He Visits His Uncle

Three brothers shared the world when Kronos fell:
Zeus became Sky-Father, and Poseidon ruled
the deep earth-shaking waves; the underworld
was ceded to a darker god, invisible

to men, whose name is rarely spoken. Hades
dwells in shadowlands where no sun ever shone
except the midnight sunlight of the Mysteries.
Men call him 'Nourisher', the 'Wealthy One',

the dread Lord of the Dead. Beyond the dismal
fields of asphodel his stronghold lies, and not one
among the deathless gods will enter that abysmal
palace … except his nephew Hermes, Zeus's son.

The family connection lets him pass between
the worlds, a one-way tour guide to his uncle's hall,
wearing the hat that renders him invisible
and lets him enter daylight sight unseen.

He Takes up Divination

When Hermes asked Apollo for the gift
of prophecy, the older god declined
to share his right of access to the secret mind
of Zeus. 'Be lord of sheep,' he said, 'and theft;

and try to learn a thing or two from bees.'
Hermes was out on Mount Parnassus when,
while puzzling how to call up prophecies,
he watched three nymphs drop pebbles in an urn;

then dreamed up runes and the *I Ching*. Disguised
as Odin northwards, eastwards as King Wen,
this footloose and inventive god devised
such worldwide oracles as these so men

in quandaries might dial up the universe
for hints on how to cope ... or try to find
out what the gods are up to secretly behind
the scenes ... only to get things wrong again, of course!

He Giveth Tongue

Surely it takes a god this versatile
to dream up language? He must have watched
dumb mortals grunt and point before he matched
their daily needs with eloquence and style

by putting words into their mouths. And then
all babel was let loose. Once taught to speak
the glib ones found innumerable ways to tweak
the truth of things, as poets and liars, admen,

lawyers, politicians, journos, novelists.
And just to complicate the case, Hermes
invented polyglottal possibilities to tease
the world into confusion. Still he broadcasts

means of fabulation: he's the SIM card in your phone,
your satnav's voice, your texts and Twitter, webcam,
broadband fount of knowledge and the source of spam …
and he'll still be laughing when all's said and done.

He Monitors Its Use

Hermeneutics – just the kind of oblong word
for which the god, whose name it nabbed, invented
dictionaries. He can mouth them, yes, but soon gets bored
by such abstractions, and has long lamented

ever having let the literary theorists have their way
with them. He thinks plain speech a subtler means
both to enlighten and deceive. He'll spill the beans
on heady obfuscation, says that words should say

exactly what they mean, particularly when
their meaning is ambiguous – e.g. in poetry,
which speaks its sense and yet voluptuously
eludes the intellect. But weasel-speaking men

and those who dare to sanitise atrocities
with anodyne abstractions are the larger target
of his hatred and contempt. He won't forget
the way they counterfeit divine proclivities.

He Does Zeus a Favour

Argos Panoptes, giant with a hundred eyes,
two of which are always gaping wide,
is perfect, Hera thinks, as bodyguard
for pretty Io, whom she's hidden in disguise

as heifer – just to put Zeus off the scent.
Zeus isn't fooled, but puzzles how to get past
Argos, then recalls that Hermes has a taste
for escapades and is *invisible*. An elegant

solution: give the lad the nod and Argos bites
the dust. Yet gentle Hermes, wondering why
he'd take up giant-slaying just to gratify
his dad's insatiable lust, procrastinates …

until he realises that an ever-active mind rules out
imagination's chance to dream. Such gung-ho
need for close control is paranoid. And so
he aims his wand and – *zap!* – all hundred eyelids shut.

Half-Brothers

for Jules Cashford

Where is the habitation of the gods
if not in us? And where are we if not
inside the mysteries they perpetrate
about us and around? They are our moods,

our motives and the forces pulling us
apart. Also the hemispheres that live
inside the skull whose duty is to strive
to hold contraries together ... And thus

while Apollo dazzles in bright sunlight
Hermes prefers to glimmer in the dark;
each knows which best illuminates his work –
sun's constancy by day, the variable moon at night;

but Zeus shows favour to neither son. He allows
full liberty of scope to each half-brother.
Like rules and mischief, logic and smart hunch, he knows
that Hermes and Apollo need each other.

He's There at the Start of the Trojan War

The air is rarefied on Ida's sunlit peak.
The light is hard to breathe, the drop is steep,
and Paris has been guided there to keep
his date with destiny. His knees feel weak

before these naked goddesses. But, *Keep your nerve*,
smiles Hermes. *No, there's no way to play safe.*
(He knows this youth is gambling with his life
in choosing which divinity to serve.)

Hera is comely, promises power and wealth,
earth's bounty, banquets, comfort, bling;
Athena looks much sterner, yet her offering
of wisdom could prove good for mental health;

but Paris hankers after sex and beauty in a wife,
and so – no contest! Aphrodite wins … There is
a fourth who's overlooked, and Hermes knows dark Eris
is behind all this … (NB, the meaning of her name is 'Strife'.)

His Sense of Irony

All wars, he thinks, exemplify betrayal –
of compassion, human decency and trust;
though, yes, they are ignited by impersonal
intrusion of the gods in human life – their taste

for power and sex, their readiness to activate
the lust, the rage, the fear in mortal men,
and their lamentable desire to satiate
their darker drives: e.g. when Paris abducts Helen,

giving warlike Agamemnon righteous reason
for the profitable sack of Troy ... For his part
Hermes, who has seen this coming from the start,
decides it's time to double-cross such treason.

He shapes a Helen lookalike, which Paris
takes (poor fool) to Troy. While Hermes carries
Helen off to Egypt, Paris doesn't know that he
will let Troy burn for no more than a phantasy.

Daimon

'Character is destiny,' says Heraclitus:
to each of us a daimon is assigned
to guide our soul. Ignore it and we find
the fate to which that choice incites us.

Sometimes Hermes will forgo his godly role
to manifest as daimon. Wandering
this world invisibly, he brings along
his scales to weigh the balance of each soul.

And thus, at Troy, he watches while brave Memnon
fights Achilles, knowing the outcome will reflect
the strength of trust between each daimon
and the soul it's striving to protect.

Hermes himself stands intermediate
between life and death, weighing two souls
in the impartial balance of his scales.
Their tip will match each fighter to his fate.

The Whisperer

Psithyristis. He's the whisperer.
Psst! You hear his surreptitious presence
in the name, or when a sudden silence
falls in conversation and the air

hangs watchful and we say we sense
an angel pass. He is the messenger
who texts us sometimes ... may prefer
to leave a call ... but at his most intense

an urgent whisper to our inner ear
will counsel us, or warn; and if we're wise
we'll heed. That whisper is the voice
of waking dream: *Are you quite sure?*

Is that decision sound? Don't board that plane!
This will have consequence. You're sleeping
at the wheel. And if you're hoping
that he'll go away, he does ... The doubts remain.

He Escorts Priam to Achilles' Tent

Then what could Hermes say to Priam while he led
the old king and his ransom wagon through
the Argive lines? What comfort for a man who
surely knew Troy finished with brave Hector dead?

Such knowledge sits much deeper in the heart
than in the brain: the grieving king was wise
enough to see the end of things, to recognise
that, even guided by a friendly god, the cart

he'd loaded up with gold would buy no more
than Hector's corpse. What silent Hermes knew
was this: the king must kiss the hand that slew
his son to learn the true futility of war;

in that frail kiss Achilles will have lost
all taste for glory; and while both concede
ten years of slaughter waste, only the dead
across that windy plain can quantify the cost.

Stone Pile 1

Herma: a heap of stones such as a traveller
sweating in the noonday heat might make out
shimmering in the haze, then feel his dry throat
freshen at its signal that a spring is near.

And having drunk and put a random stone
on to the pile, might he then wonder whether
others who have placed an offering on that cairn
have also caught a glimpse of Hermes standing there?

Stone Pile 2

And sometimes he'll be seen at crossroads where a grave
or gallows stands: a herma marks the spot
of that excruciating zero point where what
is now becomes what's next as quantum waves

of choice shift everything. In that respect
see Oedipus and Robert Johnson – two whose
lives turned tragic (one through blindness, one through blues)
at places where such double crossings intersect.

His Gifts to Pandora

Where did it begin, this pained misprision
between men and women? How did evil infiltrate
the world? What happens when we die? To date
we've found no answers for such questions

other than in myths we credit – stories
that give meaning, order, value, to the raw
events that shape our lives. It's Hermes' law
to take a wretched situation like Pandora's

and make the best of it we can. Created
out of clay, ordained by wrathful Zeus
to work his will, that lovely first of girls set loose
the host of woes to which mankind was fated.

But Hermes offered hope, and chose to give
her cunning, a deceitful tongue, and wiles;
and if those gifts seem mischievous, how else
in such a man-shaped world could she survive?

The Night Visitor

He is the tutelary deity of night,
close kin to burglars and to writers and to those
asleep in cardboard boxes on the street.
He oversees the drowsy and the comatose,

has heard the chimes at midnight and will
act as prison visitor to those for whom
the lonely stretches before dawn become
the penitentiary of mind. His skill

at slipping between worlds will open
access to the hidden regions where
our dreams reside. Made welcome there,
he bids the sleeping soul draw deep upon

its store of images. And then, as lover
of life's pleasures, he'll reduce the space
between two sleepers into close embrace
and work his phallic magic under cover.

He Honours the Hospitable

As god of wayfarers he knows that pilgrims need
a place to rest at night, the friendly hospitality
of strangers, giving shelter, food and drink, a bed –
a common act of charitable B&B

you'd think. But once when Zeus and Hermes walked
on foot through Phrygia, putting kindness to the test,
they found the region of Tyana's doors shut fast
in their tired faces. Comfortable people baulked

at entertaining them … until they chanced across
the lowly cottage in which Baukis and Philemon
lived and loved. The couple made them welcome
without knowing they were gods; so grateful Zeus

transformed their cottage to a temple where the law
of hospitality was kept. And then, when Hermes saw
the couple wished to die as one, the god agreed to bind
them at their death into an oak tree and a linden intertwined.

He's Rated Triple A

Access All Areas: that's how,
as god of boundaries, he's rated.
He holds a universal smart-pass — so
no roadblock, razor wire or gated

private street can keep him out.
He won't be stopped by border guard
or cops, will nonchalantly flout
all travel regulations, then be guide

to legal or illegal immigrants,
to refugees and whistle-blowing fugitives.
He'll do his best for hapless vagrants
and be there for anyone who lives

like him and feels the power of his name;
but every child that drowns in the attempt
to flee a war elicits his profound contempt
for human meanness, and our silent shame.

He Considers GUTs and Such

He likes it when we hanker after truth
in things, yet smiles to see how serious
we are in postulating theories
of everything (e.g. the thoughts of Alan Guth

on quantum fluctuations in the vacuum,
Dawkins on genes, Karl Marx on history,
and imams or the Pope on God). For mystery
abides whatever postures we assume,

and Hermes knows the universe expands
each time we think we've got the explanation.
Not this, not that, but both, or maybe none
of the above, his tricksy wisdom understands

what unassisted reason often fails to see:
the tongue can't taste its buds; the only snake
to swallow its own tail does not mistake
itself as literally true … and nor, he thinks, should we.

In Dreams …

for Anthony Stevens

Artemidorus, I recall how once
you almost wept when speaking of
the animals and ancestors that nightly
gather in the darkness of our sleep
to mourn for us and for the ruin
we are making of their home.

And then in laughter aimed against
yourself you told how once in Greece
you boasted that Asklepios would come
to you in dream. He did, and shot you wide
awake in shame at his rebuke for using
him to prove your ego's point.

For nothing speaks more truly than a dream,
and where else (asks Hermes), in the jangle
of a time so fast to change that even
wisdom seems redundant, shall we keep
those secrets that the soul discloses
for our welfare while we sleep?

Hermes to Odysseus

'So in your dream the blind seer said, "Walk inland, far
from freedom of the seas, until you come across
a figure waiting for you, who mistakes the oar
you carry for a winnowing fan. There kiss

the earth and make your offerings to the god –
a full-grown ram, a bull, a breeding boar –
and where the ground runs dark with blood
of holy sacrifice, there plant your oar."

And who was waiting for you there but me,
your timely friend who long since recognised in you
the grandson of my son Autolycus, the three
of us all kindred tricksters, wily spirits who

are footloose, restless, fugitive and free …
Yet how that night it made my wild heart laugh
to watch you sort your heart's wheat from the chaff
and let your navigator's oar become a tree.'

His Private Life

Does he have lovers? Yes, but he's a fly-by-night
whose sleek allure seduces nymphs with whom
he'll have some fun, then leave. He'll never mate
for life — his lightfoot ways allow no room

for serious commitment ... And yet once
he went back to Kyllene working as a shepherd,
where he fell for Dryop's daughter, fathered
goat-horned Pan and grew to love this shaggy prince

of flocks and lonely places. And then another child
was seeded inside Aphrodite one wild night
when their hot genes conceived the first Hermaphrodite
in whom contending opposites are reconciled.

Says Cicero, 'some writers of more secret texts'
opine that even love child Eros was his by-blow
on the virgin Artemis! Perhaps ... but only gods can know
the darker mysteries of love and sex.

His Role as Psychopomp

What can the deathless ever know
about the strict and non-negotiable
fact of death? Hades, in that dark hall
to which the shades of mortals go,

has 'knowledge of all noble things', and death's no
stranger than the timeless climate of the place
he rules and rarely leaves. But in the case
of Hermes things are different. Although

himself immortal, he is the close companion
and friend of those who have just died.
At their last breath he's present as their guide
into the underworld of Hades' dark dominion,

and must on each last journey surely feel
some empathy for human fear and grief?
If so, perhaps, as kindly friend and clever thief
it's just their grief and fear he wants to steal?

The Missing Hermes

for James Simpson

These days we see his simulacra everywhere
in con-men, paparazzi, adverts, junkmail, spam,
on Twitter, email, texts from mobile phones. (Beware,
though, when your broadband crashes from some scam –

that 'teenage hacker' could in fact be him.)
Doubly deceptive, such imposters imitate
the trickster god, but who would raise a hymn
to praise their names or gaily celebrate

the guile that keeps their motives hidden?
Hermes is irreplaceable, and yet scarcely seen,
in this cold time, consorting with the maiden
nymphs who keep the waters clear, the landscape green,

and are the triple-natured form of she
who is, as Demeter or Hecate or Gaia,
the mother of it all. Her Green Man, son and lover, he
belongs right at her side, in matter – and in maya.

Hermes Redivivus

for Patrick Harpur

Common as muck: so said the alchemists
about the raw material they worked to make
their philosophic gold. It still exists –
you'll find it everywhere, it's there to take ...

but it's intangible. Its heat won't burn;
its water won't make wet. It is the star
in man, the secret fire, that treasure
of great price, which yet gets prized by none

who deem such paradoxes spurious.
Only a double vision opens on a world
in which base metal can be turned to gold
because it's subtly guided by Mercurius ...

who is shape-shifting Hermes in full flight,
alive again, returning from the underworld inside,
somewhere between mind and matter, playing hide
and seek ... until he switches darkness into light.

His Moon Dance

His cave birth and his piebald cap (half-black,
half-white), his fickle nature and the darksome
name by which he's sometimes known – 'the one
who sees by night' – all these bespeak

a deity whose province is the moon.
Small wonder then the alchemists once knew
their sly Mercurius as 'Heaven's dew'
and 'circle of the moon'. For there is none

among the gods more subtly prone
to dance the passage between light
and dark, and trace the phases of the night
until day dawns again. And still he dances on,

and those he draws into the measured paces
of his dance must meet the challenge
shining from his shifting faces –
to show how life renews itself through change.

HIS OPUS

(A brief guide)

'Make the fixed volatile and the volatile fixed'

1. Nigredo

As Apollo once told Rilke: 'Time to change!'
So Hermes slips into the vas hermeticum
and starts to decompose. He'll now become
whatever time and alchemy arrange.

Inside the magic jar the sky is moonless.
He plunges into darkness after dark,
and will remain a raven trapped by night unless
he perseveres with this black work

that may, at any moment, fail.
He is the jar, its murky contents, and
the alchemist, and neither truly male
nor female but an ampersand

that twists between the two, in process.
He's pitchblende slowly turning into tar,
yet even in the deeps of this distress
he's on the lookout for a single star.

2. Albedo

Like sun at midnight, look – the morning
star appears. The jar is gleaming white,
and all bleak shadows spawned by night
disperse inside this new day's dawning.
Hermes now knows himself Hermaphrodite.

Two fountains pour into a single bath
where all impurities are cleansed away,
and so he shimmers into joyous day
as Lucifer, redeemed by patient faith
that matter is the stuff of soul at play.

The raven's gone. He's whiter than a dove,
a deer, a unicorn; but he's not finished yet.
His Moon is gleaming but the Sun's above
her head. They're not yet intimate.
Until they bond, the work is incomplete.

3. Coniunctio

'Separate; coagulate': such is
the golden rule of his spagyric art.
First analyse the mass in pieces,
then bring together what's been torn apart.

He finds that his Sun and Moon, the King and Queen,
are contraries that must be reconciled
before he can be whole again,
and, from their union, a child

conceived to bring the promise of new life.
So he declares a royal wedding shall
be held to change him into man and wife.
All are invited to the festival

where, in his thalamus, the naked pair
unite in warm embrace to make
that golden third – the joy of mutual desire
which now transfigures him for love's sweet sake.

4. Rubedo

His inward light becomes celestial.
He dreams of lions, phoenixes and fire, the glow
of body heat in gratified desire, and how
bright Luna as the shining bride of Sol
has made his mind responsive to his soul.

What once was fixed in him was rendered volatile
and now what's volatile is fixed. Day breaks,
and all the world is waiting as he wakes
to birdsong while the colours of the peacock's tail
spread open round him. Naked, quick and virile,

Hermes steps out into the golden dawn
to feel warm sunlight glitter in his blood.
His flesh glows ruddy as a rose. Newborn,
all one, alert, alive, this shifty god
has now transmuted into perfect Stone.

His opus ends; the dance goes on.

His Emerald Tablet

Time doesn't mean a lot to gods. It's just
a theatre of entertainments where
the mortals strut their stuff and swear
that they believe in gods, or don't, and cast

about for stories that make sense
of their short lives. Worshipped or ignored,
the gods endure, are sometimes bored,
but never doubt their own divine existence.

So Hermes moves about through time,
as happy scamming with Odysseus
as being hailed as Trismegistus
by the alchemists. His patience is sublime

because he knows – his Emerald Tablet says so –
it's *all One*, and everything above
will always mirror what goes on below
while Sun and Moon are indoors making love.

Trickster

Why does this shadow-dancing rogue engage
us so? And how come we so often fall
for those who will betray us? Does the soul
require some element of subterfuge,

some ruse by which the ego is deceived
to let its self-deceptions get laid bare?
Hermes is just the god to clear the air
that way, but should this trickster be believed?

Why not? Truth is at best ambiguous –
its opposite can be some other truth –
and Hermes passing between life and death
knows what, perversely, may be best for us

however strongly we resist its claims. He's wise
to shadows in the soul and is the fitful flare
that lights our way. Cryptic and oracular,
he is the witty celebrant of mysteries.

He Takes Off

for Sebastian Barker 1945–2014

Beyond sleep and waking, life and death, he flies
into that elusive space that opens up where
fire and water, heavy earth and weightless air,
and all such opposites are reconciled by his

sublime imagination. No irritable grab for facts
or reason there, so Keats admires his Capability,
Blake approves his double vision, and STC
top-rates his Agency as prime. His lunar syntax

pleases Mann; Yeats sees him perning in a gyre;
Jung, pondering mysterious conjunction,
appoints him god of the transcendent function;
while Shakespeare hails him as that Muse of Fire

which elevates us heavenwards lest we forget
we too are visionary creatures – versatile
and contrary, perverse, benign and fallible –
and no one's got our Hermes pinned down yet.

His Wand

The god in the louche hat, the liminal,
crepuscular and volatile grand master
of quick whispers and shady deals, can pull
deft tricks and optical illusions faster

than the pixels shift in CGI. He seduces us
and mystifies our senses with his wand,
the Kerykeion or (latinate) Caduceus –
that snake-twined staff he carries in his hand

to work such vivid magic as draws doves
from darkness or releases some poor captive
from a cabinet of knives. What he loves
best is to astound the mind with such deceptive

art as brings about true transformation,
and it's the virtue of his wand to wide-awaken
into lucid dreams of the Imagination
those who don't yet see we are myth-taken.

Envoi

A body and a soul is all we have.
The body's destination is the grave.
The soul? Who knows? Mine bids my heart believe
the only remedy for life is love.

Is anything more difficult than love?
These half-rhymes are the best reply I have,
and though full rhymes may lie beyond the grave
right now my friend is dying, so I grieve ...

Yet Hermes, winking, bids me rise and dance
for all that's joyful in this mortal life,
for friends and children, and a loving wife,
and all that Hermes brings of happy chance.

And so, Lord of the Threshold, deathless friend
who guides us into Otherworld ... O keep
me loyal to the soul that wakes in sleep,
and lead me gently homewards at my end.

NOTES AND
ACKNOWLEDGEMENTS

Tetelesmenoi Hermei: 'initiated into the mysteries of Hermes' – a term used on the island of Imbros in ancient times and carved on to the grave of Karl Kerenyi in Ascona, but used here in tribute to my friend John Moat, whose many meaningful encounters with Hermes throughout his lifetime are recorded in his privately published memoir *Anyway* ...

Koinos Hermes: 'the loded stone' refers to 'lodes' as in veins of mineral ore found in rock, in this case gold because this stone is the Philosopher's Stone of alchemy.

His Conception: A fuller and more beautiful account of Hermes' birth and early adventures will be found in the Homeric Hymn to Hermes as translated by Jules Cashford (*The Homeric Hymns*, Penguin)

An Alternative Version refers to the archaic Hermes Agathopoios ('he who makes things good', i.e. fertile), who was sometimes figured as an ithyphallic stone.

His Darker Side: Autolycus will become grandfather to Odysseus, who inherits the family talent for cunning and deception. More famously, perhaps, he appears in Shakespeare's *The Winter's Tale* as 'a snapper-up of unconsidered trifles'.

He Cocks a Snook at Nietzsche (and Philip Larkin): Friedrich Nietzsche wrote powerfully of the Apollo/Dionysus duality in *The Birth of Tragedy*. In *Hermes: Guide of Souls* and elsewhere Karl Kerenyi championed

55

the Hermetic vision as a third configuration in the complexity of human experience. Philip Larkin once wrote dismissively of 'the myth-kitty' as a played-out source of verse.

He Takes up Divination: Odin (Germanic Wotan, identified by the Romans with their Mercury, the equivalent of Hermes) was the Norse god who was given a vision of the runes after a nine-night shamanic initiation (*Havamal*). King Wen, honoured as founder of the Zhou dynasty, was credited with the arrangement of the 64 hexagrams of the *I Ching* and their appended judgements.

He Does Zeus A Favour: 'Panoptes' means 'All-seeing'. Aeschylus gives a version of this story in *Suppliant Women*.

He's There at the Start of the Trojan War depicts the Judgement of Paris, who was led by Hermes to the top of Mount Ida where he had to decide to which of the three goddesses he should award the golden Apple of Discord. Inscribed 'To the Fairest', it had been thrown among them during the wedding of Peleus and Thetis by Eris, sister of the war god Ares, because her name had been omitted from the guest-list. For a fuller account see my novel *The War at Troy* (HarperCollins).

His Sense of Irony: In his *Palinode*, the lyric poet Stesichorus of Sicily (c. 640–555 BC) tells this myth of the phantasmal Helen, in which the beautiful woman whose abduction supposedly caused the war at Troy was – rather like the weapons of mass destruction in Iraq – never actually there. H.D.'s lyric sequence *Helen in Egypt* (Carcanet) explores the myth at length wonderfully.

He Escorts Priam to Achilles' Tent: In the *Iliad* Homer tells how, at the command of Zeus, Hermes disguised himself as a youthful Myrmidon and guided King Priam through the lines of the Argive army besieging Troy in an attempt to ransom the body of his son Hector, who had been killed in combat by Achilles.

56

Stone Pile 2: It was at a crossroads that Oedipus encountered and killed the man he did not yet know to be his true father. Robert Johnson, regarded by many musicians as the father of rock and roll, was reputed to have gained his musical prowess as a blues singer and guitar player in a deal done with the devil at a crossroads. Perhaps that 'devil' was Papa Legba, the Voodoo god of crossroads, close kin to Hermes, who was, after all, the inventor of stringed instruments.

His Gifts to Pandora: In the *Works and Days* Hesiod tells the story of how Zeus, who wished to inflict punishment on mankind for the theft of heavenly fire by Prometheus, commanded Hephaistos to create the first woman from clay. When the gods arrayed her with gifts, Hermes gave her the name Pandora ('She of Many Gifts') and accompanied her as bride to Epimetheus, the brother of Prometheus. Once the storage jar containing the gifts was opened, out flew all the evils that afflict mankind. Only hope remained. Much later, when Erasmus misread 'pithos' (a jar) as 'pyxis' (a box), his translation set loose the timeless cliché of Pandora's Box.

He Honours the Hospitable is based on a fable told by Ovid in *Metamorphoses*.

He Considers GUTs and Such: GUT – Grand Unified Theory, a current ambition of physicists to reconcile the presently incompatible laws of gravity and quantum mechanics. We still await the reconciliation of those contraries.

In Dreams … : Artemidorus of Ephesus was the second-century AD author of the *Oneirocritica*, a treatise on dream interpretation, but the name occurs here as an affectionate address to my friend Anthony Stevens, author of the indispensable book *Private Myths: Dreams and Dreaming* (Penguin).

Hermes to Odysseus: 'the blind seer' is Tiresias. In the *Odyssey* he summons from the underworld the shade of Anticlea, the daughter of Autolycus and mother of Odysseus, who reproaches her son for the grief and sorrows caused to his family by his prolonged absence from Ithaca. Both an account of Odysseus' journey to the Underworld and an interpretation of his oracular dream of the oar becoming a winnowing fan can be found in my novel *The Return from Troy* (HarperCollins).

His Private Life: 'writers of more secret texts' – 'qui interiores scrutantur et reconditas literas', from Cicero's *On the Nature of the Gods*.

His Role as Psychopomp: 'knowledge of all noble things' – from Plato's *Cratylus*, quoted by James Hillman in *The Dream and the Underworld* (Harper & Row).

The Missing Hermes: 'Maya' is the Sanskrit word for the illusory nature of the world as perceived in common experience. Usually translated as 'illusion', it might be rendered more fruitfully as 'imagination'. It derives from the same root as 'matter' and 'mother', and the double pun here on the name of Hermes' own mother and of the goddess Maia ('she who brings increase') is intentional.

Hermes Redivivus: For fuller insight into the paradoxical nature of the alchemical Mercurius see Patrick Harpur's novel *Mercurius: The Marriage of Heaven and Earth* (Squeeze Press).

His Opus offers a highly synoptic account of the complex alchemical operations in which Hermes as Mercurius was both the mysterious prima materia ('the first matter') at the start of the proceedings and the Stone of the Philosophers into which it was transmuted. I have followed the fourfold pattern of changes as attributed to Maria Prophetissa (second or third century AD). Her axiom runs, 'One becomes, two, two becomes three, and out of the third comes the one as the fourth.' In the colour sequence of the operations, the third is often named Citrinitas ('yellowing') and refers to the process of congelation. However, there are many variations on the sequence in the library of alchemical texts and it suited my purpose best to place the Coniunctio as the third stage of the work. The reference in the first line is to Rilke's poem 'On an Archaic Statue of Apollo'. The 'vas hermeticum' is the alembic in which the changes happen. 'Spagyric' is a word probably coined by Paracelsus, deriving from the Greek words 'spao' and 'ageiro' ('collect' and 'extract'), and is descriptive of the alchemical process.

His Emerald Tablet: a reference to the *Tabula Smaragdina* (Emerald Tablet) of Hermes Trismegistus, a Hermetic text, probably Arabic, dating from the sixth to eighth century AD and regarded as foundational by later alchemists. The *Theatrum Chemicum* (1613) offers this translation of one of its key lines: 'Whatever is below is similar to that which is above. Through this the marvels of the work of one thing are procured and perfected.'

He Takes Off: Keats wrote of Shakespeare's 'negative capability' as his capacity for 'being in uncertainties, Mysteries, doubts, without any irritable reaching after fact and reason'. STC –Samuel Taylor Coleridge, who defined 'Imagination' in his *Biographia Literaria* as 'the living power and prime agent of all human perception'. The phrase 'lunar syntax' belongs to Thomas Mann and was used in *Joseph and His Brothers* for 'both/and' thinking as opposed to 'either/or'.

His Wand: CGI – computer-generated imagery. 'Kerykeion' is the Greek name for a herald's staff of office – the golden wand of Hermes. 'Caduceus' is the more familiar Latin version. The author was uncertain whether the final line contained the worst pun he had ever made or the best. Hermes insisted that he let it stand.

Among books I found helpful in thinking about Hermes were: *Hermes Guide of Souls* by Karl Kerenyi (Spring); *Trickster Rules the World* by Lewis Hyde (Canongate); and *Hermes and His Children* by Rafael Lopez-Pedraza (Daimon). Many insights and images in these pages arose from conversations with my friends John Moat (author of *Hermes & Magdalen: Poems and Etchings* [Typographeum]); Patrick Harpur, (author of *Daimonic Reality* [Viking], *The Philosopher's Secret Fire: A History of Imagination* [Penguin] and *A Complete Guide to the Soul*

[Ebury]); and Jules Cashford, (author of *The Moon: Symbol of Transformation* [Greystones Press] and other illuminating studies). Her forthcoming book *The Wand of Hermes* promises to be a definitive work on Hermes as symbol of the Imagination. If truth be told, my borrowings from these friends were so influential that, were it not for their unfailing generosity of heart, they might qualify as typically Hermetic thefts. I also wish to express my deep gratitude to the poet Jay Ramsay (author of *Alchemy: The Art of Transformation* [Thorsons]) and the novelist Anthony Nanson at Awen Publications for several helpful suggestions and for placing their faith in this book.

www.awenpublications.co.uk

Also available from Awen Publications:

Places of Truth:
journeys into sacred wilderness
Jay Ramsay

Poet and psychotherapist Jay Ramsay has been drawn to wild places all his writing life, in search of a particular deep listening experience. 'Trwyn Meditations', a sequence set in Snowdonia, begins this 24-year odyssey. 'By the Shores of Loch Awe' takes us to the fecund wilds of Scotland. 'The Oak' celebrates an ancient tree in the heart of the Cotswolds. 'The Sacred Way' is an evocation of Pilgrim Britain. 'Culbone' records the hidden history of the smallest parish church in England in a steep North Somerset valley near where Coleridge wrote 'Kubla Khan'. The final sequences, 'The Mountain' and 'Sinai', takes us beyond, in all senses, touching the places where we find I and Self.

'Here is a poet who dares the big picture, writing unequivocally from the soul to the soul.' *Alan Rycroft*, Caduceus

Poetry ISBN 978-1-906900-40-3 £12.00 Spirit of Place Volume 4

The Firekeeper's Daughter
Karola Renard

From the vastness of Stone Age Siberia to a minefield in today's Angola, from the black beaches of Iceland to the African savannah and a Jewish-German cemetery, Karola Renard tells thirteen mythic stories of initiation featuring twenty-first-century kelpies, sirens, and holy fools, a river of tears and a girl who dances on fire, a maiden shaman of ice, a witch in a secret garden, Queen Guinevere's magic mirror, and a woman who swallows the moon. The red thread running through them all is a deep faith in life and the need to find truth and meaning even in the greatest of ordeals.

'In her lively and vivid stories, Karola Renard points a finger towards the mythic threads that run through life's initiations.' *Martin Shaw*

Fiction ISBN 978-1-906900-46-5 £9.99

Dancing with Dark Goddesses: movements in poetry
Irina Kuzminsky

The dance is life – life is the dance – in all its manifestations, in all its sorrow and joy, cruelty and beauty. And the faces of the Dark Goddesses are many – some are dark with veiling and unknowing, some are dark with sorrow, some are dark with mystery and a light so great that it paradoxically shades them from sight. The poems in this collection are an encounter with many of these faces, in words marked with feminine energy and a belief in the transformative power of the poetic word. Spiritual and sexual, earthy and refined, a woman's voice speaks to women and to the feminine in women and men – of an openness to life, a surrender to the workings of love, and a trust in the Dark Goddesses and their ways of leading us through the dance.

'Potent, seminal, visionary' *Kevin George Brown*

Poetry/Dance ISBN 978-1906900-12-0 £9.99

Words of Re-enchantment: writings on storytelling, myth, and ecological desire
Anthony Nanson

The time-honoured art of storytelling – ancestor of all narrative media – is finding new pathways of relevance in education, consciousness-raising, and the journey of transformation. Storytellers are reinterpreting ancient myths and communicating the new stories we need in our challenging times. This book brings together the best of Anthony Nanson's incisive writings about the ways that story can re-enchant our lives and the world we live in. Grounded in his practice as a storyteller, the essays range from the myths of Arthur, Arcadia, and the voyage west, to true tales of the past, science-fiction visions of the future, and the big questions of politics and spirituality such stories raise. The book contains full texts of exemplar stories and will stimulate the thinking of anyone interested in storytelling or in the use of myth in fiction and film.

'This excellent book is written with a storyteller's cadence and understanding of language. Passionate, fascinating and wise.' *Hamish Fyfe*

Storytelling/Mythology/Environment ISBN 978-1-906900-15-1 £9.99

Lightning Source UK Ltd.
Milton Keynes UK
UKOW02f2046181116
287990UK00004B/25/P

9 781906 900434